T0365717

Trapped by Gangs
Rescued by God

ESCAPING GANG LIFE

Dr. A.V. Strong Jr.

Written and produced by
Michaela,
Columbia, SC

Order this book online at www.trafford.com
or email orders@trafford.com

Most Trafford titles are also available at major online book retailers.

Print information available on the last page.

ISBN: 978-1-4120-6530-6 (sc)

Trafford rev. 01/02/2024

 www.trafford.com
North America & international
toll-free: 844-688-6899 (USA & Canada)
fax: 812 355 4082

A Letter from the Author

Dear Friends,

Looking back and recognizing where God has moved me from a "gang banger" to a successful male role model in my home, community, and church, I am constantly humbled. With every hand shake, congratulatory remark, and award received for the present achievements demonstrated by decisions I have chosen to make (to better my community) I am eternally grateful to God and those *he* has used to bless my life. In order to rejoice with me you need to go back with me and see what it took to make *a better way* for myself. Then you too can understand the importance and heart felt passion I have towards our youth and community in creating *A Better Way* for all. A Better Way Project Go Gang Out is not just a job it is a lifestyle.

Gratefully yours,

A.V. Strong

Forward

A.V. STRONG IS A dynamic person who understands the call of God on his life. His exceptional abilities to inspire youth in dedicating their lives in pursuing sound goals are phenomenal. His passions are to see all those who cross his path to have a life of fulfillment by providing educational resources and guidance to help bring hope and positive life changes.

A.V. Strong strives daily to live his life in every area to the greatest potentials. As a friend, businesswoman, and a pastor I attest to God's hands on his life. No matter what A.V. Strong sets out to do to better his community or any other he succeeds. Constantly giving God glory, he clearly is focused in life making it better for those who come in contact with him.

A Better Way Inc. was manifested through endless hours of work and construction as well as sleepless nights and tears shed for our at risk youth. Any one who really knows A.V. Strong can vouch he is more than a dedicated business man; he is a loving husband, a caring father, a motivational employer, and a true friend.

I encourage you to read his story and hear his heart's

cry. Find out how A Better Way Incorporated has come about. Learn about the programs and the life changing effects it has on our today's youth. Communities are affected by each individual living in them as well as visitors visiting them. Take charge today and find a better way.

Sincerely,

M.G. Thompson

Reverend

Table of Contents

Forgiving My Father

LIVING WITH ABUSE

Ask me today my thoughts on my father; I am blessed to call him a man of God. Unfortunately, that was not my previous testimony in life as a young man. My father was not a man I could honor in my heart like others have. Abuse was an every day event around my house. My father beat my mother while he treated her as she was a child. He did not respect her as a woman neither of God nor as a woman with feelings and emotional needs. In the heat of the moment of whatever triggered him to become upset (whenever he became upset), he was not able to control his rage and had no problem expressing it.

Insulting words, acts of violence, and even neglects to the responsibilities of his home was commonly expected out of him from the family. That is a shame to look forward to abuse instead of love and safety from the one who should protect you.

My father's home life reflected what preachers would consider wickedness. The irony of it all is that my father was a *man of the cloth*. Do I doubt the call of God on my father's life? "No". Do I know he did not live what he preached while I was a young boy? "Yes". Because I do and have studied the Holy Bible, I recognize that all are born in sin and have something to be free of in order to please God. Even preachers have to work out their soul salvation with fear and trembling. Still, it is not an excuse to be abusive. But I knew no matter what, God wanted me to love my father and obey him to the best of my abilities. Can you imagine a life of having to show respect to someone who disrespects your person?

It brings me no pleasure to share the heartache my father caused to all his children and wife, my mother. The pleasure I do receive in this testimonial is that later, before his last breath, my father repented and asked for forgiveness. Sometimes it helps to understand a person's upbringing to properly surmise the contributed influences during their lives.

Start of
Rebellious Nature

Many of my problems as a rebellious child was triggered by the hypocrisy I witnessed at home. My father's rebelliousness towards God's word in bringing up a loving family was the start of the rebellious nature instilled in his children. Maybe my father had been raised like that by his parents.

Maybe he really believed God wanted him to literally constantly take authority of his home through correction rather than added mercy and loving kindness. Whatever the problem was, it was a problem.

A Minister
of the Gospel

The church loved my father. After all, he was a minister of the gospel. In the forefront he perfectly performed his position as a man of the cloth. It was unconceivable the way we were treated at home. The man who preached love, forgiveness, and taking care of home had no clue of how to impart the messages into his own life.

Full of Rage

Surely many of his congregational members would have been shocked to know that their well respected preacher had moments of uncontrollable rage. I vividly remember the moment he put a gun to my head when I was thirteen years old. During one of his fits of rage my life could have been taken by a pull of the trigger. Sadly enough, when you live with day to day abuse sometimes you wish you were dead.

Life does not seem to present itself as something to strive for.

Respecting Prayer

Understanding what I know now it was probably the prayers of the congregation that sustained my family and I. Ignorant to the abuses we suffered at home they really did not know how much we needed them. To this day I respect all those who have diligently prayed for my family. The one thing I would like to share concerning prayer is that I have learned to forgive.

Forgiving my father would later be one step to recovery in turning from hard, isolated, and having no value for life to learning to appreciate people and forming bonds that would turn my life up side down. Just as hardness caused me to "gang bang", forgiveness opened me up to love people. I forgave my father on his death bed when I was twenty-two years old. It was the first time my father had kissed me and expressed love for me.

The man who had caused me great pain asked for forgiveness; and I gave it to him.

I guess all his preaching must have finally turned around and confronted him to his face. For once in his life, he took responsibility for his actions at home as an abusive father. He came to terms in resolving the matter through admitting his flaw, repenting to God, and crying out for me to forgive him as well. Tears poured down my face as I forgave him.

I wonder if he really knew how much I loved him. I understand why and how an abused spouse can love the abuser. You see, as a child, I loved the same abuser my mother did though we both were terrified.

As I mentioned before, I thank God my father repented. I needed to know my father recognized his wrongful behaviors towards me. More importantly I needed to receive his love and acceptance. When it is all said and done, we needed each others forgiveness. Paying back evil works with evil works is unjustifiable. Now it was time to start taking accountability for my life.

First many obstacles would come to test my faith and character. Did I pass every test the first time? No. But I got back up and started a fresh.

When Education Made A Difference!

No Emphasis
on Education

Education was not a top priority during my elementary and middle school years. I can imagine it is harder to raise eight children verses one or two. Having seven siblings may have added to the nonchalant attitude concerning school work being done in my home. Since there was no emphasis on education, I allowed myself to become slack in the area of learning.

Full of ambition, trouble seemed to follow me whether I initiated it or not. Due to both ignorance and out right rebellion, I did not use my ambitious nature to seek out positive adventures to involve myself. In lieu of focusing on educational values, failure was presenting itself to me in a hurry.

Learning academics was a struggle. I almost gave up. Barely making it through elementary school, I had to push my way into middle school. Discouragement came easy. No one wants to be labeled stupid. Giving up on education is not hard for children left to self educate.

I needed attention. Someone to speak well of my efforts was essential. If I could not get it at home or in school I would later find that I would get it from "gang bangers". The reward for submitting to thugs was of importance to me. Praise would follow my efforts. For once in my life I felt important. Respect is sweet.

As time passed and poor decision making increased, criminal activity became like a drug to me. Instead of stressing on homework, idol time took over. With it came bad company. At age twelve I started "gang banging". I was proud to be a "gang banger".

At that point in my life education did not really matter any more. My time and allegiance was to my new friends. Believe me; the crowd I hung around did not glory over good grades.

Through hardships brought on by myself combined with a dysfunctional home life, I was confronted with life and death decisions that needed to be made. Giving up my friends would be hard. For four years I became involved in criminal activities and was at risk for the potentials or both losing my life as well as taking another's.

At age sixteen, the decision to stop "gang banging" became necessary. Carrying a pistol combined with heartlessness started working on my conscience. An eerie feeling came over me as I realized that I may be slipping in my mind. I must be going crazy if killing innocent people seemed justifiable. Could I kill to fit in the gang life? Would I kill probably was a better question?

Taking Authority
Over my Life

Making the final decision to take authority over my life helped me make a complete turn around. Still, I had to grow up and look at the path I was headed towards and make educational decisions for myself. One of the first was to be free of those holding me back. I decided to be a friend to myself first. Then I could be a true friend back.

A Turning Point

A TURNING POINT

Disconnecting from those you love is just as uncomfortable as it is a lonely experience. After all, I loved my friends unconditionally. Going through the separation brought forth anxieties. Now at sixteen years of age I was free to learn. My time for education opened up as the time for "gang banging" closed down.

My sophomore year of high school was a turning point in my life. God blessed me with effectual teachers who were able to communicate the value of education. As the willingness to learn became a positive attribute in my life, I became a teachable student resulting with a high school diploma. I made it! I graduated high school!

Living Long Enough to Graduate

I have attributed part of the educational success in my life to teachers who accepted the responsibility to strive in giving me a good education. Feeling loved and accepted by caring adults helped me want to achieve. The desires to do well in life are a reflection of others pouring out their desires for me to do well. I gladly made it through high school.

Most people would be rejoicing in the educational success part of this endeavor. But for me, having lived long enough to graduate as well as not being in prison is part of the success in receiving my high school diploma.

EDUCATED PAST
HIGH SCHOOL

Today, not only do I possess my high school diploma, I have also earned a B.A. in Criminal Justice/ Political Science in 1985 and a Master's of Divinity in 1988. In 1989 I graduated from the Criminal Justice Police Academy held at the South Carolina Criminal Justice Academy. The year 2005 I earned a Doctor of Humanities Degree.

That just goes to show when you put your mind to achieving you will achieve. Not only did I graduate high school, I went past the required education and made something out of my high school education and life.

Woman Of Honour

THE STRENGTH OF A
GOOD MOTHER

Like my father, my mother is a native Texan. My mother, Patsy R. Strong, is partially responsible for my heart beating today. Without her love, acceptance, and nurturing I would probably be dead today. Striving to impart godliness, mom recognized I had a special calling from God in my life. Regardless of the poor decisions I would make throughout my younger endeavors, mom treated me with respect. She helped me to grow up desiring self worth and respect.

Not tolerating mischievousness, Mom's constant corrections and guidance would later in life prevail. In using wise correcting techniques, mom was able to help me understand right from wrong apart from my choices. Not always making reasonable decisions, I would be convicted by her persuasive wise counsel.

Mom religiously raised her children, maintained a clean house, and presented who she was-a godly wife with conviction. Whole heartedly believing a family should stay together at any cost, with exceptional vigor and faith, mom strived to accomplish the task. There were no obstacles (regardless of situational difficulties) that would persuade her to terminate her marriage though abuse was daily present. Her strength and courage held together our broken family.

Broken in spirit through vicious remarks and beatings the family went on. When abuse manifests, cruelty and degradation come with the package. Unaware of the full effect, my father was raising his children to have temperamental issues that would later have to be dealt with. The preaching man she loved, the anointed by God man she married who was supposed to bring forth joy, peace, unity, harmony, and spiritual healings crumbled the spirits of those he resided with. Nevertheless, my mother was selfless putting others first. Determined to keep her sanity in the Lord, she pursued to persuade us to do the same.

HOME ABUSE
DISCOVERED

At first she tried to hide the home life distresses. But as the abuse progressed, it was also discovered. Our home life would become common knowledge to more people than my parents wanted. My mom sacrificed her own happiness to insure her family's. The only way to describe my mom is with a question asked in the bible. Proverbs 31 asks, *"Who can find a virtuous woman? Her price is far above rubies?"* Mom is most definitely priceless. It also talks about a wife not doing harm to her husband. Even though people were becoming aware of the abuse situation, my mom held her peace and said nothing derogatory about my father.

Mom is blessed above all women in my life. She has been a strength, comfort, and mentor. She has been there for me at all times. I can with all earnestness say I love my mother because she has helped me to partially understand the unconditional aspects of love. Love is more presently felt after you have done wrong. Anyone can love you when you do right.

"Mom's Labors of Love are not in Vain"

Even though Mom endured extreme abuse inflicted by my father, she kept the family together. In spite of the constant degradation infringed on her she showed love and compassion by not leaving him. In no way can I tell people to stay and put up with the abuse. I have pondered in my mind if holding it all together was produced out of fear of my father or faith towards God. Regardless, Mom operated in mercy and raised her children to the best of her ability as a whole family unit.

The pleasantness of a mother's love can not be totally surmised by fluffy words. My mother was a true housewife, homemaker, and parent. All the nurturing and care that can be expected from someone who loves you is present in my mom even today. She listens and prays for her children. Cooking, cleaning, organizing, and presenting an environment of safety is what I saw my mother do while living at home. She is still one of my best friends today. The sad thing about people who go all the way to make other's lives successful is the lack of gratitude shown while they sow seeds of love.

Even though mom's labors of love are not in vain,

like me, all of my brothers and sisters experienced seasons of trouble in their lives. Yet, we are not defeated. The blessing of successful marriages with loving environments is proof of answered prayers resulting from cries out to God from my mother. I have learned to modify much of my home life by pattering after the virtuous characteristics of God presented to me through my mother as well as having listened to ministerial sermons presented through my father.

After my father passed away, my mother started enjoying the life she was not formerly able to partake in during my father's living days. Mom was blessed to travel and decide for herself the future she would strive for. It is a shame that these opportunities had to come so late in her life. But what is really important is that these opportunities came. Whatever I can do to enhance her happiness I will do to the giving of my last dime.

My Mother, Patsy R. Strong

Murder Through Gang Violence

Rival Gang Murder

Michael was a carefree sort of character. He lived for the moment making decisions at a whim. Gang involvement was his lifestyle. Unfortunately what he loved to affiliate himself with would be the cause of his life being wasted away in such horror that I have to fight not to hate when I think about it.

Michael was a straight out thug. Even though he had dreams and ambitions like anyone else he did not respect anyone. Like all "gang bangers" the respect they think they have for themselves is quite disrespectful. Due to poor life choices he paid for his decisions. Michael was kidnapped by a rival gang and beat to death by a baseball bat.

One of the perpetrators verbally repeated the scene while on trial. He described the violent acts the rival "gang bangers" imposed on Michael. He stated that after striking Michael in the back of his head with a baseball bat, a hole was created by the blow. As Michael's brain started spilling out of the hole the *rival gang* then proceeded to urinate in his face as they watched him die.

Gang violence took the life of my younger brother

Michael. He would never come home again. I was so sickened by the testimony it sent me running out the courthouse. I was looking for justice to prevail. I wanted the murderers to be punished.

You would think that after the pleasures of murder carried out confessed to by the rival gang, and thereafter the event was brought to court that the legal system would impart fair judgments against the rival gang members... What is fair when a life is lost? How many years can a person serve for brutal, premeditated murder? I am here to tell you, after those "gang bangers" received a six year sentence they actually only served eighteen months of the time sentenced. It taught me that *black life* was cheap.

I have another brother I am praying for that is strung out on crack. Drugs have become his outlet. Disappointments are hidden behind a high. I am hoping that he will wake up to the opportunity of change and plunge towards success. I lost one brother to murder by the hands of thugs. Loosing another brother is not an experience I look forward to.

A.V. Strong Jr. with brothers Michael (murdered), and Troy

Other
Siblings

A part from the traumatic death of my brother Michael and the heartbreak of witnessing Troy playing Russian roulette with drugs, I have an older brother named Gary and a younger brother named Chad. Like me, they are ministers of the gospel. We all struggled with identity having lived through abuse. Through our willingness to learn God has brought forth clarity and purpose in our lives. We are hoping Troy will become drug free and experience the purpose and meaning of life available to him.

I also have three sisters. Each of them is married with children. Opal and Patricia are currently living in California with their husband and families. Renitia is living with her husband and family in Arizona. I rejoice in their successfulness in raising functional families.

Childhood Gang Life

INFLUENCED BY VIOLENCE

Growing up with violence conjured up by my father's unwillingness to rationally resolve life issues contributed to my delinquent behavioral growth. The influences of bad decision making were prevalent in my life. Not receiving affections from my father hardened me as a youth.

No man, woman, or child can blame any one person for their insubordinate behaviors and actions. But, I can tell you first hand those other peoples actions towards you sure do contribute to your behavioral process. Being raised with violence in the home, anger emerged from within causing bitterness to set in my heart.

Violent behavior became a matter of choice that I welcomed. Becoming actively involved in the gang arena was one of the worst decisions I have made. But at that time it was the only one that made sense. After all, when you are with other gang bangers there is a feeling of love and brotherhood. Safety was important to me. Would not it be for any child? They had my back and I had theirs.

BLESSED INTO
THE GANG LIFE

Shortly after being blessed into the *Bloods* sect, I took pleasure in initiating other youth into the gang life. The rank of the *junior Blood sect leader* was one of my special achievements. As a proud *Blood*, I felt powerful and respected. You know how teachers feel special over the abilities to change lives through education, so did I. I helped recruit and teach others to be a part of something special to me- a *Blood*.

It was at the age twelve that I decided to go full fledge into gang activities. Shooting pistols, fighting at a whim, and watching lives taken were a part of the norm. It would not be to long before my attitude started shifting. One by one, I watched my friends either be taken away through the court system or death.

Let me elaborate on kinds of experiences youth encounter through gang activities by sharing some of my past. Once at a party I was faced with the horrifying turmoil of watching one of my closest friends die in my arms.

"LITTLE RED, LITTLE RED, THEY STABBED ME! "

Dwight was seventeen years old when he staggered out of a home we were partying at. I was already outside as he exited while crying out with screams. "Little Red, Little Red, they stabbed me!" he screamed. You could see the shock and horror on his face. There is no description of the feeling of knowing death was knocking at my friend's door.

My nick name at that time was *Little Red.* Dwight came to me, collapsing in my arms, as his blood shot out of his shaking body. We wrapped sheets around him hoping to stop the bleeding. There was no preventing the flow of blood that was escaping his body. Our efforts failed.

He closed his eyes and slept. The rival gang had stabbed Dwight in a major artery causing the blood to pour out to fast. It seemed as though the ambulance came to slow. There was no helping him regain life. Neither we nor the hospital would be able to revive him.

Retaliation followed the deadly episode. Gang wars started in the streets. I would later suffer another near loss. Yet another dear person to me would be punished for my partaking in gang life activities. Our rivals, the *Crips* ended up targeting one of my family members. My uncle suffered severe abuse by the use of a golf club. They almost beat him to death in an alley with the golf club.

It resulted in him being hospitalized for six months due to being put in a comma over the ordeal. Again there was yet another reason for a gang war. The *Bloods* had a reason to attack the rivals. A wild night of shootings took place after the perpetrators were found.

"SHOOTINGS HAD BECOME A COMMON PLACE IN THE COMMUNITY."

Gang violence was taking over. For safety and protection, joining a gang seemed to be a reasonable solution. During my teen years "gang banging" was a way of life that became normality for the youth around me. Shootings had become a common place in the community. In comparison to the necessities of life, I would have to say carrying a handgun was just as necessary as carrying a pen or pencil to class. I knew I had to do it; I needed a weapon for protection.

Reflecting
Back

Reflecting back into my childhood the park was a place of memories of experiences shared with other junior *Bloods*. I love the memories of playing basketball, joking around with my friends, sharing conversations, and knowing that the people I chose to be my friends loved each other enough to be willing to give their lives for each other.

Memories I care to forget would be the ones of blood spilled through shootings, stabbings, and beat downs. Imprisonments of friends, lives lost through gang rivals as well as the quality of life lost through paralysis due to gang violence would plague my mind.

Personally I had suffered a switch blade stabbing which barely missed my arteries. Reminded by a scare, I survived a pistol shot in my stomach. I scarcely avoided my head being taken off by a machete. On top of that, I can not even count the times I have missed death through drive by shootings.

I remember a particular day at the park where we junior *Bloods* met. I was sitting next to one of my *Blood brothers* on a bench. Someone drove by shooting at us while passing by. It all happened so fast. The shots to my friend's head ended his life. The fact of the matter is, even though the gang life confronts you with constant life and death situations, you really can not be fully prepared to lose your life nor witness the loss of your friend's.

My *Blood* brother was gone. Why did my friend have to die? Why is it that I kept being spared? Getting tired of all the shootings, I became emotionally distraught. I was appreciating life with the added blessings of friendships. Loosing friends by the hands of rival gangs was getting old quick. What can I do now? Do I hold my head up high and proud in the name of the *Bloods* or hang it down low in knowing I lost a friend? After all, my valued friend would no longer be a comfort to me in this life.

"It was like violating
the sacred trust."

Gang wars have their restrictions and boundaries. I remember retaliation after a rival gang shot at my neighbor's house while in the process of acting out a drive by shooting. The door of the house was shot off, barely missing my neighbor's mother. A lesson would have to be taught. The nerve of them not considering his mother's safety.

When engaging in gang combat there has to be some type of respect. It was common knowledge that during shootings, stabbings, fist fights, drive by shootings or uses of any other weapons during rivalry attacks there was the restriction of hurting and taking out (killing)the mothers. Mothers were honored and well respected. To hurt a mother was like the ultimate form of disrespect. It was like violating the sacred trust. The perpetrator would be dealt with harshly.

...FIVE CARS...WITH LOADED PISTOLS

You would think by now that I would have learned my lesson. How many people close to me would have to be hurt or killed before I would see the light of the fruit of my own activities? Another party, another shooting, another retaliation would come. A young lady named Pam had a party that resulted in yet another shooting.

There was a shootout and Pam got hit. What a misfortune for an innocent person to be the receiver of such an unwanted gift of a lodged bullet for the exchange of entertaining youth. A bullet severed her spinal cord; paralysis immediately followed. To this day Pam is still paralyzed. Her misfortune combined with the other misfortunate downfalls of gang life started affecting my conscience. Who would think I had one?

Was I becoming soft? At this point, thoughts of getting out of the gang and living a more simple life was definitely an option worth looking into as far as I was concerned. The only problem presented were the hindrances of knowing what happens to those who "punk out". Believe me, those thoughts were not comforting.

I had to protect myself. The only thing to do now was to go with the gang and take vengeance against the rival gang for hurting Pam. In my heart I was tired of all the shootings. But what could I do? We did what we had to do. We loaded up five cars full of *Bloods* with loaded pistols. We were on a mission. Somebody was going to pay. Somebody was going to die.

While preparing for what would be the biggest shootout of my life, I could not help but think on the stupidity of all this gang violence. I was really fed up with all the fighting, gang colors, and shootings, deaths, and ridiculous rules. God must have opened up my eyes; all blood comes out red. This killing spree is nonsense.

As we drew nearer to our war destination we drove by my father's church. Compelled to stop I ordered the car to be halted. We separated from the other four cars destined to fight a bloody war. My Blood brothers looked puzzled as I got out of the vehicle and approached the church. Not knowing what to do the others followed me into the church. The church was having a revival. My Blood brothers and I sat in the back. I found peace sitting on the pew. My mom looked back to see me sitting in the church. Overwhelmed by my presence, tears flowed down her cheeks. My mom had been praying for me to get saved and leave the gang life. Getting me into church was a start.

My father was preaching a message on "the protocol son". Somehow I knew I was just like the boy who left his home with the comforts and safety to be mischievous. My wasted potentials had played its toll in my life. In my heart I knew I was ready for a change. During the church alter call I was drawn to the front of the church as a metal object is drawn to a magnet. Not only did I commit my life to Christ that day, but so did four of the other *Blood brothers* with me.

The fifth *Blood brother* with us had decided to leave the church and join the others in rivalry. Donald, Reggie, Dionne, Laurie, and I would later find out that by our being in the church, we missed a bloody massacre. The one who did not stay with us regrets it to this day; he is serving a life sentence in prison. Nine of our *Blood brothers* were murdered in the massacre.

God is so good. He used me, the one who recruited and helped train others to do violence, to bring the same people to church to help them save their own lives from blood shed as well as save their souls. I owe my life to God; so do they. We have become brothers all over again. This time we are brothers in the Lord. The only fighting we need to do together is in fighting the good fight of faith.

Thank God, through all my shooting spiels, in my

knowledge, I did not take a life. Prison could have been my place of residents today. Death could have called me home early. I saw the end of crime life through other's sorrows. Reaping their end was not my idea of receiving the appropriate reward for all my efforts. Neither jail nor death was my goal.

Evidently a new plan for success needed to be implemented; the one I followed was not appealing anymore. Common sense finally kicked in. Looking back I am reminded of the message my father preached on the protocol son coming to his senses. Let us just say I came to mine.

Willing To Punk Out

WILLING TO "PUNK OUT"

Taking responsibility for my actions became easier as new friendships developed. Humbling myself to self disciplines in studying, I earned an education. The more I learned the more I understood that the most powerful weapon is education. Positive changes followed me as I submitted to authority. I found a place of peace with myself to do well.

This change in attitude was all self fulfilling; but in order to achieve, I had to be willing to "punk out" of the gang. Showing me as Christian became a new way of life. Truly, I was a new creature in Christ. Prior life skills and decisions were turned around to do good rather than evil. New positive decisions towards education manifested. Even so, I had a pit in my stomach concerning the walk to school. The day after the bloody massacre, the day after I said yes to salvation, I would have to cross the familiar park to get to school.

The thoughts of the parks history of gang shootings flickered in my mind. How would I cross the park alive after leaving the gang? I had to be able to walk across the park. How I used to dodge bullets with my friends while trying to play ball. There had to be a look out person while we played ball. At the time they spotted rival cars pursuing the park they would warn the rest of us and we would take cover in order to dodge bullets fired out of the weapons aimed at us. There was no fear of being shot at because it became normality. Knowing when to take cover was the major focus.

Getting to school in one piece was my present goal. My mom knowing the dangers of leaving the gang wanted to drive me to school. I was not a coward when participating in the gang; becoming a coward now was unacceptable. The possibility of death or a beat down alarmed my senses. Jesus gave me reasons to be free and go forward. The comfort of knowing my life was now in God's hands stirred up faith inside to do what was suicidal to others-confront my ex "gang banging" *Blood brothers.*

When I gave my life to Christ, I gave him my trust as well. Scriptures my mother quoted to me empowered me to go by faith. She told me God has not given us the spirit of fear and that no weapon formed against me can prosper. Either God in all his realness would prove his word to me or my present reasons for being would be diminished. I had to be able to face my past, walk in the present, and take authority for my future.

Declining my mother's offer and making the walk

facing those I both loved and abandoned ended up being one of the best decisions I have ever made. As I approached the *Bloods* I could see the hostility of a former *Blood brother*. His piercing eyes reflected hatred as he drew his hand up to beat me down. The decision to go to school was already made. I only had to live to do it. I had already made up in my mind to die for what I believed in.

Thank God the O.G. (original gangster) stopped the hit. I was spared the pain and agony of physical abuse. At the mercy of the O.G. he decided to help me instead of allowing a brutal attack against my person. He knew my life and my allegiance had been to the *Bloods*. He must have perceived on behalf of me "punking out" there had to be a powerful influence. Rumors of my salvation went before me. The O.G. knew God was that higher power. God had showed out again. He turned the heart of the O.G. towards my good and not only blessed me not to be beat down or killed, but from that day forward the *Bloods* escorted me to and from school as ordered by the O.G. My safety was insured. I no longer had to wonder about my former *Blood brothers* turning on me.

Consequently, I was the first to graduate high school out of my family. College was no longer a far away dream. It had become a reality. Even my former *Blood brothers* showed up to my high school graduation. The prayers of the righteous do prevail. To all those who prayed for me I am eternally grateful.

Escaping Gang Life

MARRYING HIGH
SCHOOL SWEETHEART

* My heart full of love and thanksgiving for a young lady who listened to my pain filled stories with a compassionate ear provoked me to propose marriage to her. With all my heart I believed my decision to marry at the young age of nineteen was appropriate. Do I regret the marriage? No. Marrying my best friend and sweetheart Karla was convenient. What we would come to regret were the unresolved issues of my childhood that would plague our relationship.

To be honest with myself and everyone else, I grudgingly have to admit one of the primary motivating factors in walking down the isle was the need to prove to my dad that I was a better man than he. Driven to show him how to be a husband and family man, anger was more prevalent than loving affection on my end of the marriage. Here my best friend, my sweetheart, my wife, would have to endure my need to put my father in his place.

Married, I needed a new environment and a new means for life. I was the man. Responsible for my wife's well being I realized the old crowd and familiarities of daily events had to change. She needed to be safe and provided for. The military was a door to fulfill the endeavor.

MILITARY SERVICE
FROM 1977-1998

Realizing God had blessed me to live in spite of prior "gang banging" activities and even after jumping ship by getting out of the gang life, I became thankful for my blessings. Continuing to achieve in obtaining a good education followed by a high school diploma was an added touch. Now to top it all off, I had a beautiful, caring, compassionate wife who loved me. This was living. I was doing it right.

Though I turned from a criminal lifestyle, many "gang bangers" I had ran the streets with still kept me as a friend. The reality of their lives possibly being taken by bullets tore at my heart. In order to totally be free of sentimental connections I would have to move. The military became my way of escape. I had to take this open door of opportunity for my wife. It was time to step up and be a real man.

Initially, my desire was to play football. As an accomplished high school football player several offers to play football in a variety of college universities followed. Then the unthinkable happened. Injuries to my knees disqualified me in qualifying for the athletic scholarship which previously was made available. My doctor would not give me the needed waiver to pursue the promising football career I yearned for. Reluctantly, the doctor would agree to produce a waiver to allow me to join the armed forces.

Newly enlisted in the Army, I packed my bags and headed for Georgia. Surviving boot camp became a new goal. Toughened by gang life as well as life experiences I would successfully complete the mission. Vigorous training did not compare to the strain of being lonely. Away from my wife, I dwelled on my past. Not having spent any length of time away from home made the time away seem longer. Depression was starting to have its way with me.

BASIC
TRAINING

The military promises multiple choices of benefits in travel, education, work skills, family assistance, housing allowances, medical, dental, retirement, etc. Why should I be upset? What is there to be sad about? Not having all the answers, I came up with my own solution in being free of the depression. I decided to self medicate through the use of alcohol.

Traveling oversees, separation anxiety set in. Being away from family and friends was more than I cared to handle. It is hard to stand alone when you have had your homeboys backing you up. Mom was there when they were not. And then there was my wife. Loneliness in this capacity was new to me. All the benefits presented by the military could not keep me smiling. Attending church was a routine I continued in though I no longer strived to live holy. Consumed in grief, I consumed myself in the bottle.

Putting aside the vows made to my wife, I indulged in the pleasures of other women. I knew I loved her; I just went from one extreme to another in my pursuit to happiness. No woman could please me enough to be free of the depression. It would later take an act of God to free me of the demons within. I did not love God as he loved me.

AFTER THE OVERSEES TOUR (AWAY FROM MY WIFE)

Even after my wife and I were able to be together I continued in my selfish ways. Knowing I was not the same man that left before the tour I tried to hide my drinking problem. It would be on a particular day, while outside, my two year old daughter would grab my cup full of soda; one of my hidden flaws would be revealed. Thinking she was going to drink the soda which had secretly been mixed with alcohol I snatched the cup out of her hand. My wife immediately suspected there was something wrong. It was normal for my daughter to drink out of my cup.

My wife found out that day I had been secretly drinking. The alcohol was hidden in a secret place in the car. Not expecting to get caught, I ran and poured the alcohol into my cup while no one noticed. Shortly after the escapade more severe depression followed. My moral was low. Depressed, I stopped caring about the things most important to me. Even God was on the back burner. Still prayers to God parted out of my lips. I depended on God to be there even though I stopped going to church and serving *him*.

Hiding my family problems from my own self I put all my efforts into my career. Flourishing in my military career, I had stood proud making rank. Opportunities for further promotions were made available. I worked with generals and other high ranking officials. My uniforms were starched and pressed with perfect creases. I presented myself as a clean cut proud soldier. While attending drill sergeant school the struggle to conceal my drinking problem was becoming more unbearable. Fear gripped me. If I was exposed, my military career could be in jeopardy.

As much as I loved my wife, giving up other women was not an option. My state of mind increased from one level of darkness to another. The price of infidelity finally caught up with me. My wife left. Somehow I knew it was only going to get worse. You may not understand or even want to understand I really loved my wife. Believing I had done better than my father in being a husband I tried to justify my actions. After all, I did not beat my wife!

WAKING UP

I remember driving in my new car. The gas was on empty. Five dollars in my pocket I continued to drive. The car broke down between the liquor store and the gas station. This would be the final moment of truth. Would I take the money to purchase the well needed gas; or would I continue to drink my sorrows away? Between you and me, you know I was actually creating more sorrows every time I made the choice to drink away the pains of growing. Making the final decision, I parked my car on the side of the road and left it. The liquor store won my prized cash amount of five dollars.

Concerned, my friends confronted me. They knew it was not my character to behave so bizarrely. My problem had come to a head. There was no more hiding it. Face to face with what I had become I sought out help. I had lost my wife and family. I would risk loosing my friends and military career if I did not change.

Remembering what God had done in sparing me from the hands of gangsters, I called on *him*. Prayer put me back on the track. Restoration followed. My wife came back. God showed out again. He blessed me. This time I could never turn my back on God again. I have been faithful to *him* ever since.

Leaving
Active Duty

After leaving active duty I joined the reserves. Promotion followed me once again. I had to refuse re enlistment into active duty military in order to keep my family together. God had given them back to me. It was up to me to keep the blessing. Re enlistment would have produced another tour separating me from my family.

During my term in service I was a squad leader during the Grenade War in 1983. I would later be called to battle in 1990-1991 to participate in battle at Desert Storm while in active duty reserves. I served approximately nine years as a reservist from 1989 to 1998. While assigned to Fort Jackson Army Base, I served as a senior drill instructor for three years. Also, during my enlistment at Fort Brag, I operated in law enforcement as a military police officer in the 5th Special Forces Unit.

Receiving medals and honors during my military service included the areas of Good Conduct, Merit Service, Three Oak leaf Clusters.

OLDER AND WISER

Older and wiser, I still go back to the same picnic table at the same park were my old friends hung out and dodged bullets from rival gangs during my younger days. Constantly praying for the safety and salvation of those who still live among us, I am obligated to minister to those I left behind. God has given me an earnest longing for their success in this world. If I can change, anyone can. I hope their remembrances of my past lifestyle are combined with memories of my present achievements that they also may believe for positive changes to happen in this life time.

God has really revealed this is more than a story of a person flipping back and forth from bad to good, good to bad. It is about *him* taking a broken boy and making that same boy whole through *his* power. All these blessing came because a young boy learned to cry out to God and believe his mercies are new every morning. Again, at his weakest moment in adulthood he reapplied the same principals achieving the same results. Be encouraged in your time of need to be free to ask *Him* for help.

Upholding The Law

Ironically, I went into a career field no one would have perceived me venturing into. God blessed me to go from one extreme to another. I went from studying the ways of the streets to studying the ways of upholding the law. Who would have guessed an ex "gang banger" would transform to a law enforcement official? But that's what happened.

During the thirteen years of working in law enforcement, I worked for both the Columbia Police Department and the Richland County Sheriffs Department. My responsibilities and titles were patrol office, school resource officer for both C.A. Johnson and Keenan high schools, and undercover narcotics officer. I also worked on the gang task force.

The most troublesome moment in law enforcement happened after a homicide investigation. Shots were fired. One person was down (hit by a bullet). There were two bullets lodged in the victim's chest. He was seconds from death. Despite of what took place two youth ranging from ages eight to ten were standing around eating hot dogs. They happily gave each other a high five slap to the hands when I heard one of them say "Dude's not going to make."

Reality
Check

My eyes opened up to the insensitivity of the youth surrounded by violence. That day was a reality check for me. Though I had lived a young life of violence I had justified it as being a way of protection from the opposing rivals. After realizing my poor choices I changed. Truly, I was alarmed at the lack of concern for life as the youth continued to eat their hot dogs as if they were in some type of popcorn theatre watching a movie scene.

These youth had no remorse pertaining innocent lives being taken. Death did not frighten them. Bullets shot out of weapons did not scare them. Their reactions were similar to those who watch a neighborhood fist fight and are glad to see the one down hurt. The word homicide meant nothing. The youth have been desensitized. This world is in for trouble. Something has to change.

· Later, while pondering the events which had taken place throughout the day, with frustration in my voice, I tearfully cried out "There has to be a better way." Flashes of my younger brother's murder haunted me.

I was in a stupor. Life was not making too much sense right then.

I needed some kind of guidance. Wanting to make a difference in the lives of youths, I needed a plan. My heart filled with both rage and sorrowfulness towards the attitudes of the youth. I searched for some type of solution to the matters. I would get my answer. Something miraculous was about to transpire.

The answer came to me in a sudden blast. As God gave me the vision I wrote it down. That night the *Gang Out* program for A Better Way was written as the revelation divinely poured into my thoughts and heart and then onto the paper I wrote on. There is no doubt in my mind of God blessing me with the vision. In the Holy Bible the book of Habakkuk gave instructions to write down the vision that the reader my run with it to accomplish the goal.

The Lord blessed me with a heart for the youth to see to their educational needs concerning street life verses law that they may have a better way. Through education their choices in life would be broader and presentations would be made available which would help persuade the youth to be law abiding citizens. They had to be taught the consequences of breaking the law beforehand as a prevention technique. They also needed to meet others seeking to help youth succeed by offering specialized services.

A Better Way, Project "Go" Gang Out launched off. Finally, there was a program available that was not comparable to any other for the children of South Carolina. So many appointments were requested that I could not keep up with the schedules. Later, I would have to hire those equipped to speak for the program to go forward in the community and disperse the well demanded information.

After receiving constant requests to present gang identification information throughout the United States including Canada, I traveled more frequent as I ventured to varieties of sites in Washington D.C., Florida, Chicago, California, Georgia, North Carolina, Philadelphia, New York, and throughout South Carolina.

ORDAINED BY
GOD

In my eyes upholding the laws of God was just as important as upholding the laws of the land. Dedicating my life to God, I studied theology and God's principals learning to both apply them as well as impart them. Having proved myself before God and man I was ordained as a minister of the gospel.

Pinehurst Community Center allowed me to use their facilities to hold youth events, cookouts, and festivals. The vision was to bring alternatives for drug uses and bad decision making by providing positive and motivational outlets for the people of the community. I sought to do all I could to reach the lost including reaching out to the people of Hendley Homes and Saxon Homes where I was able to start a drug prevention program helping low income families.

While providing services in the Saxon Homes area I was also able to implement a baseball team which incorporated more than just coaching. It was a way to mentor the local youth in team building, anger management, and character skills. Juanita McDonald aided me in launching an exercise program which brought added joy to my heart. Physical fitness has always been a part of my life whether it was through gang activities, military life, or law enforcement duty. Applying myself to the best of my abilities, I set out to give back to the community. Thinking about it was not enough. It's my duty before God and my country to be a blessing.

A.V. Strong Jr. with Mother and his children

*A.V. Strong at Calvary Cross Church of God in Christ
/Teen Dinner*

Planning A Better Way
Project "Go" (Gang Out)

THE ORIGINAL PROGRAMS OF A BETTER WAY, "PROJECT GO"

A Better Way "Project Go" started off with the Lord implementing a program in my mind which I put on paper. January of 2001 was the year the program initially started. While still active in law enforcement, I had to juggle time between home, church, work, social, and the new program.

After dedicating myself to the task of carrying out the vision of A Better Way Inc., I found a couple of people (Xavier McDaniels and Keith Bailey) to support the vision. Xavier "X" had played for the New York Nicks, the Boston Celtics, and the Seattle Super Sonics. He was known for his outstanding defense and scoring abilities. He became a primary spokesperson for A Better Way Incorporated. Keith Bailey, a retired army military soldier, who presently is a County Councilman in Blythewood also committed to representing this new grassroots organization. Both Xavier and Keith Bailey helped round up the initial youth whom participated in the *gang out* program of A Better Way Inc. They also were the primary financial supporters of the program (buying tee shirts and food for the at risk youth).

The need for this new program was evident. Successful changes were taking place in our community through the youths' acceptance of A Better Way "Project Go" (Gang Out). As the program grew the need for additional volunteers grew with it. Having gone door to door to offer our services, an increased number of interested youths and families of at risk youth (by gang activities and/or drug activities) resulted.

TROY HARWELL

In the fall of 2002 Troy Harwell joined the staff. He came on board and jumped right into mentoring the *gang out* youths. He currently participates as a group leader helping our youth at risk to set goals and make positive life changes. Troy motivates our youths through classroom assignments which incorporate leadership and life skills. His showing of unconditional love helps our youth to open up and participate with open discussions. He has given freely of his time and efforts. I appreciate his steadfastness and longsuffering through the task of training and retraining our youth in coping with today's society.

Troy Harwell also has a burden to help the youth enjoy life. He has put smiles on our youth with Christmas gifts he has freely given for the past two years. His teaching abilities are well appreciated at A Better Way Inc. He has been a consistent positive male role model for the past three years.

Valerie Hodge-Sample

Valerie Hodge-Sample, founder of Positive Image Consulting in Irmo, South Carolina, was one of the most influential inspirational motivators rooting for the work God had started in me to become a success. We started off in an old leaking building not caring about the dripping water. Our primary objective was to see the youth in our community get the help they needed.

When working with youth you have to see past what they may or may not deserve and look to give them what is required to make positive decisions.

Sonjia Howard

Shortly there after Sonjia Howard, a LMSW joined in as a volunteer for the *gang out* program in November 2003. She later became the Program Manager for A Better Way Inc. where she still holds that position today. Sonjia also operates as a counselor providing services to individuals, families, and age appropriate groups. Sonjia Howard has a stable work history as a social worker on Fort Jackson Army Base in South Carolina. As a professional certified counselor she also operates as an entrepreneur owning her own counseling business. Next to me she currently is second in command for A Better Way Inc. Her grant writing abilities has been a well needed asset in the growth process of A Better Way Inc. Sonjia assisted me in modifying the program design used to promote A Better Way Incorporated.

Sonjia Howard's professionalism is backed up with both her educational and work history. She has held positions such as the Lead Clinical Counselor for Lexington/Richland Counties Drug and Alcohol Commission were she conducted staff training and development, and Program Coordinator for S.C. Department of Alcohol and Other Drug Services were she managed the program for adolescents in the juvenile justice system. As a social worker for the South Carolina Department of Juvenile Justice she provided direct social work services to incarcerated youth and provided supervision to master's level student social workers. She conducted assessments and treatment plans as well as provided direct services to individuals and families while working as an intensive family therapist for the South Carolina Youth Advocate Program. Sonjia also has provided treatment and supervision to youth residents who are victims of abuse/neglect as a Therapeutic Counselor for Carolina Children's Home.

Sonjia holds a Master's of Social Work from the University of South Carolina were she has also operated as a Research Assistant. She has also earned a B.S. in Psychology.

THE ORIGINAL PAMPHLET
FOR A BETTER WAY INC.
READ AS FOLLOWS:

A Better Way, "Project Go" Positive **activities that guide midlands youth through the high teenage years...**

A Better Way, "Project Go" educates and empowers misguided youth and their families by helping them reach their full potential, leading them from a destructive path to *A Better Way of Life...*

"Project Go" believes that troubled youths need positive intervention, treatment, and responsible adult influences to become healthy and productive citizens of our community.

Participation in A Better Way "Project Go" is confidential. The information in the program will not be shared with any agency or organization unless permitted by the participant.

Far too many youths in the midlands area have no goals, few dreams and no stars to reach for. *A Better Way "Project Go" w*ants to change that. *"Project Go"* is an intervention and prevention program designed to create positive activities for youth that are at-risk and following a destructive path within their lives.

A Better Way, "Project Go" works with teens and their families experiencing problems related to violence, negative peer influences, gang-related behavior, truancy, and other self destructive behavior.

The founder of *"Project Go"* was both a former teen gang member and police officer. Out of those experiences he created a program to address the specific challenges teens and their family's face that are at-risk of becoming a tragic juvenile crime statistic.

"Project Go" along with the support of local Churches, schools, and other community programs works to provide positive outlets for teens and a support system for their families.

A Better Way, "Project Go" Programs

- **Gang Out (Youth Intervention Program)**
A prevention and intervention program for potential and/or current gang members, associates, and their families interested in leaving the gangs.

- **Parents Helping Parents**
An empowerment program for parents and family members coping with the stress of raising at-risk children. The program provides counseling and referral services for the entire family.

- **Go A Better Way!**
A youth leadership development program that instructs teens on character development, self-esteem building, and positive leadership skills through interactive activities and cultural field trips.

- **Project Go Community Education Program**
Provides workshops to Churches, schools, and community groups interested in learning information on the threat of gang related violence in their community and within their families.

SYLVIA KENLEY

Sylvia Kenley, the current Volunteer Mentor Coordinator of A Better Way Inc., had previously performed her internships with both A Better Way Incorporated and in a low level residential treatment center for recovering drug and alcohol addicts on Platt Springs Road in South Carolina. I met her in the year 2003 during her first visit to the *gang out* program. She fell in love with the God given vision of A Better Way Incorporated and has been involved ever since. Her prior experiences in counseling addicts have enhanced her abilities in mentoring children with addictions. She had previously been employed in a mental health facility for a consecutive period of eleven years.

Her passions for youth provoked her to complete two years as a Guardin Ad Litum where she visited children placed in foster care. Her experience in investigating families for the best interests of children she was assigned to monitor has sharpened her senses in recognizing varieties of abuse issues.

Currently she still represents children at court hearings in regards to home placements for children at risk for abuse. Sylvia has also operated as the Program Manager for OBGYN for the State of South Carolina in the Primary Care Division of Physician/ Medical Services for the past three years. She left her full time job with all its included benefits in October of 2004 to dedicate herself in helping at risk youth in South Carolina. Her passions for youth can be traced through programs she actively participated in such as coordinating the summer camp program for Camp Sunshine at Colonial Christian Academy, working with youth in ministry, assisting in mentoring youth in New Life Books' mentoring program, and coaching youth basketball.

Due to a tragic drowning accident (which took place over four years ago), Sylvia lost here husband. This unfortunate event has opened her eyes further in seeing the need for additional mentoring support in the homes of single parented children. A Better Way is there for her children. Her daughter Auja C. Kenley has also joined A Better Way as part of our youth staff. She assists in taking attendance, greeting those who participate in our programs, and is a peer mentor.

As the titled Volunteer Mentor Coordinator, Sylvia Kenely is the first paid employee of A Better Way Inc. She has filled in many shoes including operating as the office manager, a volunteer office trainer, a mentor for children of prisoner's trainer, a public speaker, and a gang out staff member.

A product of University of South Carolina, she holds a B.A. in psychology. She also earned her Masters in counseling from Webster University. There is no value you can put on the lives of those who give up the fame, glory, and benefits of job positions to be available to give back to the community. Sylvia is a light in this world.

MICHELLE G. THOMPSON

Sylvia J. Kenley's initial visit was to fill in for her sister Michelle Thompson who was unable to attend due to an overloaded work schedule. After time was made available to visit A Better Way's *gang out* program, Michelle made her way in and like wise fell in love with A Better Way Inc. At first it was hard for her to swing two jobs and be free to actively participate at *gang out*. But, like her sister Sylvia she had a passion for our at risk youth. She took a leap of faith and decided to put her career goals aside and make a difference in her surrounding communities.

Michelle's fifteen years of work experiences with youth have prepped her to effectually reach children at risk. She had previously taught in both Mount Zion Christian Academy in Durham, North Carolina and in Colonial Christian Academy in West Columbia, South Carolina. As an ordained minister she has fifteen years of ministerial work experiences including teaching, preaching, evangelizing, pastoring, and publishing Christian materials. She has worked with youth in Ohio, North Carolina, and South Carolina in a variety of youth ministries. As a Christian business owner she has implemented a mentoring outreach program for both youth and adults through her business. Her abilities to both listen and teach unconditionally have enabled her to effectively communicate with the at risk youth.

After a few visits to our *gang out* program Michelle decided to get involved. She first volunteered as an office worker typing, answering phones, and taking messages. Her life experiences have prepared her to step in and be flexible in a variety of tasks. She has operated as a motivational speaker in bringing awareness for the need of A Better Way Inc. in the local communities. She has worked with youth and interns as a kitchen supervisor and has worked with clergy at Camp Bethel Christian Camp along with Sylvia Kenely, Auja Kenely, Dominique Thompson, and D.A. DeAndreA during A Better Way's summer camp retreat in 2004. Without prior notice she has been able to step in and go places and speak to recruit mentors for the children of prisoners as well as mentors for gang out and/or speak on A Better Way's programs. She also is one of our trained volunteer mentors for children of prisoners.

When I had to go to Washington D.C. both Michelle Thompson and DeAndreA Walker filled in for me at the Call for Care Conference speaking before clergy including Dr. Tony Evans and community leaders which included Mayor Stan Shealy and House of Representative Chip Huggins whom gave both A Better Way Incorporated and staff a favorable report during my absence.   Other panelists were Sheriff James Cannon, Sherriff Leon Lott, community leader Henry Bracy, Pastor Heanon Tate, Minister Margaret Harper, Reverend Joseph Jennings, Officer D.A. Coles (City of Columbia), Attorney Mike Easterday, and Police Chief Timothy Ford. The Call for Care Conference was hosted by the Dr. Tony Evans, Dr Stephen Manley, Christ Central and Mrs Gladys Grimaud of the City Light Coalition.

D.A. DeAndreA

DeAndreA better known as "the black Mexican" joined A Better Way staff the first week of March 2004. Though A Better Way Inc. is presently renovating a building off North Main Street in Columbia, South Carolina, we still hold our weekly gang out program at Friendship Baptist Church where DeAndreA usually opens up the meeting with prayer and a scripture reading. Not only is DeAndreA a minister of the gospel, he also is a mentor, a group leader, a public speaker, and a gang awareness presenter. DeAndreA has both escorted and assisted me in my travels to publicly speak to parents, communities, community clergy leaders, and schools while performing gang presentations.

YOUTH MENTORS

Michelle's daughter Dominique S. Thompson also has joined the youth staff and is a positive youth role model along with Auja Kenley and Brittany Scott. Brittany Scott is dedicated in representing A Better Way Inc. She has actively participated in gang awareness presentations in a law class at A. C. Flora High School. After successfully completing the *gang out* program Brittany stayed on to work as a junior staffer.

Both Auja Kenely and Dominique Thompson are currently published for writings they have submitted. As successful students in high school they have been asked to be published in the next addition of the Who's Who of High School Students. Though they both have a history of honors including invitations to leadership trainings for outstanding young achievers, they walk humbly before their peers.

Dominique Thompson's achievements are numerous including receiving the Best Female Actress Award in 2004 for a dramatization performed at Benedict College in South Carolina were she had a leading role. She has also been filmed in a variety of Kids Now programs and was a part of a televised production in promoting Christian churches to unify. She has also won a writing award which placed first for the Lt. Governor's Writing Award from Lt. Governor Bob Peeler. She wrote in comparison to children's' abilities to forgive verses adults'. She hoped adults would be more like children. Her clean record, public speaking endeavors, and academic achievements are a plus as a young role model for our youth today. Dominique also helps prepare food for A Better Way Inc. during our *gang out* sessions.

The talented Auja Kenley successfully is in her sixth year of orchestra where she plays the Base stringed instrument. She currently is in an inspirational club at Airport High School which deals with today's female issues titled the Women of Tomorrow. Auja is also actively involved with the student government.

Current Programs (Operating) Through A Better Way Inc.

A BETTER WAY
INCORPORATED'S
CURRENT VISION IS:

MISSION STATEMENT

We promote healthy living by educating and demonstrating positive alternatives and reducing the likelihood of "at-risk" behavior among youth and adolescents to encourage their maximum potential for success in life.

VISION

We strive to make a difference in our children, our families, and our community through continuous "best practices" education, training, empowerment, growth, and enrichment for youth, adolescents, and their families.

Program Description

A Better Way Inc. is a 501-C (3) non-profit organization specializing in the areas of prevention and intervention for reducing "at-risk" behavior among youth and adolescents. The program provides an array of services and opportunities to children and families. Stakeholders are those whom desire to make a difference in the lives of our future (our children), our families, and our communities. The ultimate goal of our agency is to assist, develop, teach, and implement coping strategies for children and families by providing information and tools to teens and their families who desire to change their behavior.

INITIATIVES

- Project GO (Gang Out)
- Mentoring children of Prisoners (MCOP)

SERVICES PROVIDED

- Training and Educational Workshops
- Psycho-educational Groups
- Parent Connection Support Groups
- Mentorship
- Individual, Groups, and Family Counseling
- Forums and Age Appropriate Groups
- Behavior Modification
- Cognitive Behavioral Therapy
- Rational Emotive Therapy
- Alcohol and Drug Educational Groups
- Coping/Life Skills
- Recreation
- Service Learning Opportunities
- Summer Job Opportunities
- Community Referrals

A Better Way's Project "GO" Gang Out program works. It's geared to work for those who are sincere about changing their life styles. We get into the hearts and the heads of our participants to help surface the root of the problems they are faced with. Even though God gave me the vision to initiate A Better Way Incorporated, I knew it could not be a one man job. There were needs for counselors, mentors, office workers, kitchen workers, clean up crews, drivers, motivational speakers, and other volunteer workers to fill in the areas as needed.

After finding a location to set up headquarters I needed a building to run our office through while renovations were undergoing at our new site. Gary Washington, President of Gervais Professional Suites, opened up the doors for us to set up office in Gervais Professional Suites. Knowing that I was financially challenged during that time, Gary Washington extended a generous hand of help by charging our office a discounted rate along with the benefits of in kind services which included free telephone services. Because of his generosity I was able to focus on program issues rather than financial challenges of running an office. It takes everyone willing working together to produce a successful program.

A Better Way's programs are filled with informational programs needed to reach at-risk youth and their families. We reach our youth through varieties of counseling techniques ranging from one-on-one intakes to gender and age related workshops, to family counseling sessions, to full house group functions. I could go on and on about the varieties of ways we reach our at-risk youth but it would be better for you to check it out for yourself.

YOUTH EXPLOSION

Life Giving Outreach Center's Pastor Dr. Henry A. Cleare has been a personal spiritual advisor to me. I honor him as a man of God and spiritual leader in the community. His church offers many outreach programs that reach at risk youth. Dr. Henry A Cleare started Ranluco Transitional Services in 2003. Services included training church volunteers and community-based organizations to work with ex-offenders, helping them reintegrate into society. It also offers case management services to meet needs such as temporary employment and housing. Ministering to thousands of inmates, Ranluco Transitional Services offers a reentry life curriculum.

A Better Way Inc. participated in both the planning as well as in bringing youth to participate in the "Youth Explosion" at Life Giving Outreach Center which was sponsored by Anita Olden with Ranluco. I sent Sylvia Kenley and Michelle Thompson to work with Anita Olden in planning in the areas of gift bag simulations/distributions and possible after care counseling. After three meetings with Anita Olden, Sylvia and Michelle went out in the community and received donations that made up fifty gift bags to be distributed to the foster children and at risk youth that were invited to attend the Youth Explosion program. The bags consisted of plastic cups, soaps, shampoos, note-pads, pens, cozies, and the bags themselves. William E. Lloyd, General Manager of the Travel Lodge and Troy Harwell, Branch Manager of First Financial, Michelle Thompson, President New Life Books *Mentoring* and A Better Way Inc. supplied the bags with the contents in support of this community outreach service.

Though I didn't attend the Youth Explosion my-self, part of A Better Way Inc. staff and youth did. All enjoyed the activities which included gospel singing, gospel hip hop, poetry, mime dancing, Life Giving Outreach Ministries Mime Team, Benedict College Mime Team, Award Winning Richland Northeast GAP Choir, and a skit. That same morning A Better Way Inc. washed cars to fundraise for the Check Out Da Biz Youth Festival we were going to hold on a later date at Finley Park in Columbia, South Carolina. After the Youth Explosion program, A Better Way's youth went to view a Christian movie supervised by Donovan Bryson, Sylvia Kenley, and Michelle Thompson. It was a fun filled day of activities.

Check Out Da Biz
Youth Festival

Youth today look for outlets from their day to day activities. A Better Way Incorporated gets the youth involved with their communities. Our Check Out Da Biz Youth Festival is a prime example of one event our youth were actively involved in. The Gang Out youth, A Better Way Inc. staff and volunteers along with parent volunteers worked hard washing cars on the weekends to help raise the funds needed to bring the festival to pass. Donovan Bryson coordinated the event assuming the primary role as the planner. He went throughout the community receiving donations to give away free food at the festival which was held at Finley Park in Columbia, South Carolina April of 2005. Over twenty Christian acts were performed by singers, dancers, musicians, step teams, rap groups, mime teams and award winning song writer "Eddie B".

Our youth felt as if they were partly responsible for bringing about an event they worked hard to see come to pass. It's a joy to see youth glad to work to give back to their community. They enjoyed walking around the park, dancing to the music, singing, eating, and just watching the events of the day. When it was all over, they were still smiling. That's success. Even though we wanted more participation than what showed up on that windy and partially drizzling rainy day, we did not let it stop us nor the performing acts from having a good time.

In the end we were convinced we would do it again. After all, it's not about the crowd; it's about reaching our youth. Our youth applied themselves to accomplish a task and came out on top.

Aquysha L. Arthur's "TRY" Program

There are many people in this world that are serious about making a difference in the lives of others. After speaking with Aquysha L. Arthur, I was convinced she was one of those unique individuals. I met Aquysha through a network meeting sponsored by Midlands Technical College where I had the privilege of being a primary speaker. Through that meeting Aquysha L. Arthur and I started networking together.

I am thrilled she has come aboard and performs her teen pregnancy prevention program "TRY" (Teens Respecting Yourselves) with our youths at A Better Way Inc. Aquysha's "TRY" (Teens Respecting Yourselves) program, which she is the founder and executive director of, teaches self esteem issues as well self respect in respecting your body. She encourages both our male and female youths to not allow others to come in and invade their bodies sexually by making a comparison to not allowing others to come into their homes and vandalize their property.

Not only does Aquysha L. Arthur teach our youths abstinence, she also teaches consequences in being sexually active. It has taken Aquysha approximately a year and a half to get to the place she is now in mentoring youths in these areas. She started the "TRY" (Teens Respecting Yourselves) program because she had wished there was an effectual program operating in the same areas of need when she was a youth. She wants to offer the community what it did not offer her at a young age. After trying various programs none measured up to what she felt would effectually discourage sexual activities. Many come more from the standpoint of participating in safe sex verses abstinence.

Her primary objective at A Better Way Inc. is to teach our youth to go beyond the birth control pill and condoms in controlling unwanted births. She encourages youths to visit AIDS Wards for a reality check. Her methods bring awareness to diseases being transmitted in the same manner babies are conceived. Her program instills moral values as well as brings the teens to a place of realizing the actual potentials in accomplishing any goals set. She whole heartedly teaches the youths to endure the hard times during their mental, physical, and emotional change periods in order to achieve their commitments to themselves. The effectiveness of her program is a result of her constant guidance and encouragements. Aquysha is one of the many qualified individuals mentoring our youths at A Better Way Inc.

Youth & Adult Program Testimonials

The following testimonies are written letters to A Better Way Incorporated and are stored in our organizational files. Both the names of our youth and adults are protected by our confidentiality clauses. Though we have many testimonials, I would like to share a few.

A.V. STRONG, EXECUTIVE DIRECTOR, A BETTER WAY INC. PROJECT "GO":

I want to be the first to testify on behalf of A Better Way Inc. There have been thousands of youth and adults whom have received services from our organization. Hundreds of youth have given up their gang affiliations and life styles. Our program has brought awareness to current issues evolving in our at risk youth's lives. Many who have believed that gang affiliation was the best source of protection have learned otherwise. We are about bringing a positive change to all interested. Through referrals as well as voluntary walk-ins we have impacted our local community. A Better Way Inc. has launched off and is spreading its fire throughout America. We want to make a difference in America. Our children are choosing a better way of life. God has blessed the program to work. Just as education in the school system brings about success in the lives of its participants, education on preventive gang measures is a step to success for all who want this world to be a better place.

A SIXTEEN YEAR OLD MALE OUT OF COLUMBIA, SOUTH CAROLINA WROTE MARCH 2005:

"The very first time that I came to gang out was a very good experience to me. Then I got into a little bit of trouble and I came back. A.V. Strong has helped me out in so many ways I can't even explain it. Sonjia's counseling is really helping me out because now I think about what I do before I do it. Jay also helps me out because he was an ex folk and that gives me motivation to do the write thing. So even when my time's up I will continue to come to gang out and show other people the way they should go."

A PARENT IN COLUMBIA, SOUTH CAROLINA WROTE APRIL 2005:

"I have witnessed the dramatic changes in my son's attitude towards law enforcement officials as well as those he has to submit to in the public school system. When he first started at gang out he wanted to drop out of school. ... that same summer he got on the right trail and was promoted to the next grade. Since participating at Gang Out he has given up the old crowd of friends. ...He is now doing well in school, in his community, in his attitude, and in church. He started smiling again. Thank you Gang Out for all you have done through... counseling and events."

A TEEN MALE FROM BLYTHEWOOD, SOUTH CAROLINA E-MAILED THIS NOTE MARCH 2005:

"Hello A.V you probably don't remember me but me, my brother and my dad use to come to the meeting every Monday...I'm leaving this to let u know we are doing good and I am trying..."

A woman from East Clarendon Community wrote February 2005:

"I want to personally thank you for taking time out of your busy schedule to spend time and share your experiences with the East Clarendon Community. I had a chance to sit through all four of your presentations...The fact you were able to adapt to each of the audiences was great. I learned something new each time you spoke...I have received several calls from attendees and spoke with several of the teachers at the school. Everyone was grateful that you "kept it real"...You have set the alarm clock to ring; we will now be able to better handle situations that may come upon us. I believe that knowledge is power, and we must empower our youth to stand up against peer pressure and do the right thing... we are looking forward to you visiting us again. The staff at Walker Gamble Elementary, where my kids attend school, have heard wonderful things. They are excited about the possibility of you returning to our school district with follow-up presentations. Keep up the good work. We need more adults like you to look out for the best interest of our young people. After all, they are our leaders for tomorrow. God Bless You!"

Venturing Out Of The Local Community

After word got out on the successes of A Better Way Inc., many requests to perform gang awareness seminars, trainings, and meetings followed. The need to be aware of youth activities in communities both in and out of state became a priority to community leaders and fellow citizens.

I became just as involved in the local communities as I did distant.

The more the demand for travel increased so did the need for local helpers to get the Gang Out job done.

I can give you life changing events but I cannot give you names of those we have helped change due to our promises of confidentiality. Chester Middle School allowed me to perform a gang awareness presentation which resulted in fifteen students turning over their gang flags. This positive change in the youths' giving up their gang lives not only affects them; it affects their families, their communities, their schools, and those who would have suffered if they would have stayed in the gang. It prevented crimes from being committed by them because of their gang affiliations.

Clarendon County is another area positively affected by A Better Way Incorporated. Approximately fifty students combined from Clarendon County Middle School and Clarendon County High School were turned over to me after performing a gang awareness presentation. In March of 2005 Clarendon County School District No. 3 wrote: *"Dear Mr. Strong: ...I am writing this letter of commitment and support of your efforts to combat gangs in communities and schools...Organizations like yours provide a valuable resource to schools districts and communities. The increase number of gang related incidents forces schools and communities to reach out to outside organizations for support. Your recent workshop in Clarendon Three proved to be informative for teachers, students, parents, and the community. We look forward to developing a partnership with you in combating gang related violence in schools and communities."*

Just as a preacher goes out into the streets and ministers one on one to individuals as well as ministering to large groups, I have gone to the streets of Washington D.C. and spoke one on one to youth who were willing to listen to me present to them life choices that would make life easier legally.

I had flown to Washington to be a part of the Helping America's Youth program that President Bush held. I participated in one on one gang awareness issues with youth at the Community Charter School in D.C.

It brought me great joy in engaging in one on one conferences with individuals on the streets of

Jacksonville, Florida. When you have a true passion for something you cannot sit around and wait for a paycheck to motivate you to do a work needed to change the world. Money is nice, but you cannot wait for it to tell someone *there is a better way.*

Locally, I have been able to be in front of both small and large groups presenting alternative life styles to gang activities. I have had the awesome experience of being in front of approximately four hundred students at E.L. Wright Middle School. For those who have not immediately responded to the messages presented to them from A Better Way, I still believe that we have left them with thoughts and ideas that they can apply when they are ready to change. My prayer is that those who were present would hear the cry for a safe and sound community where our youth can freely understand their choices to stay gang free. I have found that many youth do not know they can get out of gangs safely. Some believe they have no choice but to join a gang for safety. Sometimes they want a better way but are afraid to stand up and let people know. I offer them confidential conferences to aide them in their transitions. By going out and presenting truth, many are able to make right decisions. Knowledge is a powerful weapon; it will take you far in life.

Strong In God

Having a heart for **God,** I became actively involved in the church in 1976. I had participated in the choir as both a singer and musician. My area of expertise was in playing the drums. Later, I would teach my son Corey to play the drums and he continues to this day to play the drums in the church. As a youth minister I ministered in various churches in my early ministerial life. As time went on, I would become an assistant pastor and then go on to becoming a full fledged ordained minister of the gospel. In 1995 I became the Pastor of Calvary Cross Church of God in Christ were I currently Pastor.

God is truly the one I have to give all thanks and praise to for all the success of my life. Without *Him* I could not accomplish anything. As I stated earlier, it was a vision from God that inspired me to write down the successful programs that would make a difference in the community. As I obeyed the small things given me, greater works manifested. Now not only do I reach individuals in the local areas but I go out of state as well. There is no limit to what man can do when we come together to perform a work that will change our nation.

I hope my story encourages you to strive for success in not letting your past mistakes determine your future successes. You to can turn away from bad life decisions and make something out of your lives as well as bless others in it. Not only am I active in Christian ministry, so is my wife and my children. My wife teaches adult Sunday school; one of my daughters, Constance, is active in church activities; and my other daughter Colayne is a church secretary. Also, my son Corey is a church musician performing on both the keyboards and the drums. Being a former drummer, I appreciate his talents all the more.

Reaching the lost is the main objective of my life. A Better Way Inc. is a part of successfully utilizing the combinations of talents God has blessed me to operate in. I dedicate my life to *His* service.

*Special Thanks in Supporting A
Better Way Inc. Go to ...*

3ᴿᴰ Annual A Better Way Inc., Project "GO" Gang Out Supporters

Hall of Fame Football Legend Jim Brown

Thanks go out to President George Bush, Laura Bush, and Antonio Boyd, for having a heart to work with at-risk youth and supporting programs generated to help them.

Special thanks go to those who have supported A Better Way Inc. Thank you:

First and foremost all thanks and praises go to *God*

First Lady Laura and President George W. Bush/supporting at risk youth prevention and intervention programs

A BETTER WAY INC. (ABW) STAFF/ VOLUNTEERS/INTERNS/ BOARD OF DIRECTORS/ PARTICIPANTS:

Keith Bailey/Deputy Director

Xavier McDaniels/ Former NBA Star/Spokesperson

Sonjia Howard/ LMSW The Change Factory/Program Manager

Melissa Pearson/ PhD Candidate/Parent Connection/ Board

Troy Harwell/ Lead Mentor/Security

DeAndreA/Minister/Mentor/Security

Sylvia Kenley/Volunteer Coordinator Mentor for Children of Prisoners

Stephanie Childress/Mentor

Donovan Bryson/Mentor/Planner/Fundraiser

Maxwell Highsmith/Volunteer/Security

Sheralet Taylor/Mentor

Katherine Andrade/Consultant

Michelle G. Thompson/Pastor/Writer- New Life Books/Mentor

Daren Myers/Mentor/Security

Auja C. Kenley/Jr. Staff

Dominique S. Thompson/Jr. Staff

Brittany Scott/Jr. Staff

Rachel Ryan/Intern- Midlands Tech. College/Mentor

Kelly Ellis/Intern- Midlands Tech. College/Mentor

Erin M. Noll/Intern- Midlands Tech. College/Mentor

Amy Ravenscraft/Intern- Midlands Tech. College/Mentor

Ashley Ellison/Intern- Midlands Tech. College/Mentor

Bobby Minder, Photographer

Eric Schinderler, Web Master

Pastor Dr. Henry A. Cleare/Spiritual Advisor

Parent staff

Volunteer Participants

Vince Ford/Chairman of the Board, Richland School District 1/A Better Way, Project "Go" 1st Annual Banquet Speaker

Steve Crocker/WIS TV, Anchor/A Better Way, Project "Go" 2nd Annual Banquet speaker

Football Legend Jim Brown/A Better Way, Project "GO" 3rd Annual Banquet speaker

Renee Alston/Fund Raiser

Carl Glover/Program Contributions

Mr. William P. Lloyd/Hildegard J. Lloyd/Program Contributions

Mary Davis/Program Contributions

New Life Books Mentoring/Program Contributions

Deacon Eddy Burton/Security

SPECIAL THANKS: Pastor Anthony Dicks Sr. / Friendship Baptist Church/Church Secretary Jackie Carter/USE OF BUILDING FOR GANG OUT PROGRAM

Camp Bethel Christian Camp

FREE PUBLIC SERVICE ANNOUNCEMENTS AND/ OR INTERVIEWS:

WIS TV

WFMVG FM 95.3

KISS FM WXLC 98.5

WHXT HOT FM 103.9

WTGH HEAVEN AM 620

Craig Melvin/Presenter Gang Out/ Radio Host/WIS 10 Television Anchor

Trey Taylor/Radio Host KISS FM/Presenter Gang Out

Chip Huggins/House of Representative

Mayor Bob Coble

Ron Thomas/Public Affairs Consultant

John Brown, Financial Services

Mr. Jim Konduraz/Sue Holmes and The Psars Foundation

Lee Adams

Columbia Urban League, INC.

Gary Washington, CEO and the Staff/Gervais Professional Suites

Mt. Nebo Baptist Church

Neil Nadkarni and the Staff/The Nurturing Center

Palmetto Health

Pastor Eddy Guess/

Pastor Norvel Geoff/Reid Chapel AME Church

Bishop Josh Lorick

Bob Johnson

Reverend Dr. Charles B. Jackson, Sr, /Brookland Baptist Church

Pastor Spry/Teen Spirit

Pastor Barbara Krell/Refreshing Springs Church

Pastor Herbert Bailey/Right Direction Christian Outreach

Bethlehem AME Church

Bishop Coulter and Judieth Covington/Missionary Church International

Reverend Joseph Jennings

Anthony Dew/Youth Motivator

Anita Olden/DAODAS

Gladys Grimaud/City Light Coaliton

Jimmy Jones/Christ Central Ministries

National Association of University Women (NAUW)

New Life Missionary Baptist Church

Bell Memorial Baptist Church

William E. Lloyd, Gen. Manager/Travel Lodge Suites, Columbia SC

(Horseshoe Drive)

Devon and Sun Harris/Juvenile Justice Ministries/ FCR Missionaries

A.V. Strong Jr., Parents

A Better Way's Check Out Da Biz Youth Festival Workers and Contributors:

A Better Way Inc. Staff - Labor

Aaron's Rental Center – Fundraising

Calvary Cross Church of God in Christ – Labor

City of Columbia Finlay Park – allowing us to rent the park

Cromer's – Equipment

Gang Out Staff and Youth Participants – Labor

Gervais Professional Suites – Fundraising

Mr. Jackson – Fundraising

Joe's Amoco – Car Wash/Fundraising

Larry Nutt – Equipment

Pastor Michelle G. Thompson New Life Books Mentoring Outreach – handing out Christian tracks/Labor

Pastor Barbara Krell/Refreshing Springs Church – Donation

S-Mart – Fundraising

Sport Plex Indoors – Donation

Ms. Stephany Childress – Face Painting

Tawanna Johnson/Who's It all About (WIAA) Staff – Fundraising & Labor

The Master's Table – Equipment

Trinity Church – Fundraising

Who Rider's Bike Club - Fundraising

Performing Acts

Silent Mime Team

Derek Presley

Disciples of Christ Evangelistic

Eddie B./Recording Artist

Hope Haynes/Poem

The Youth on a Mission

Master's Table/Recording Artists

Silent Resolution

Brother Darrius/Speaker

The Inktroverts

Life Giving Outreach Ministry

Kingdom Builders

Cross Faith

Pastor Daniel Harmon/Speaker

Bryson Girls Duet

Rachel Bryson/Poem

Donovan Bryson/Coordinator/Planner

Sylvia Kenley/Assistant Coordinator

Background Statement

A.V. STRONG

Executive Director, A Better Way Incorporated

EDUCATION:

Graduate:
Cholla High School, Tucson, AZ 1978

B.A. Criminal Justice/Political Science:
Temple University, Philadelphia, PA 1985

Master of Divinity:
All Saints College, Memphis TN, 1988

Criminal Justice Police Academy Graduate
South Carolina Criminal Justice Academy, 1989

PROFESSIONAL EXPERIENCE:

A Better Way Incorporated:
Founder/Executive Director, 2001- Present

Richland County Sheriff's Department, Columbia, SC
Gang Task Force, 1999 - 2001

Richland County School District One, Columbia, SC
School Resource Officer, 1996 – 2001

Columbia Police Department, Columbia, SC
Community Liaison, 1995 - 1999
Police Officer, 1991 – 1995

United States Armed Forces
Army Soldier, 1977 -1998

PROFESSIONAL AFFILIATIONS:

South Carolina Chapter of Law Enforcement
City Lights Organization
Interdenominational Ministerial Alliance

RELEVANT AREAS OF EXPERTISE:

- Gang Culture and Behavior
- Gang Prevention (FBI Certified)
- Dedication to community based youth advocacy
- Mentor to youth seeking an alternative to gang life

MINISTERIAL EXPERTISE:

- **Active in ministry since 1976**
- **Ordained Elder and Pastor 1983-Present**

After Thoughts

Seeing the processes and the endurances A.V. Strong Jr. has sustained throughout the process of building A Better Way Incorporated, I am a witness of the genuine character he possesses as well as the voluntary struggles he endured to accomplish the task before him. Sincerely, I am proud of the accomplishments he currently walks in. I eagerly wait to see the fruition of his present goals to both continue and to expand his efforts in reaching at risk youth.

His sacrificial nature is confirmed by his constant giving of himself as a Pastor, a friend, a fellow citizen, and a concerned Samaritan in his community. Truly, I am both blessed and proud to be his friend.

Juanita McDonald

Printed in the United States
by Baker & Taylor Publisher Services